THAT WAS THEN
Memories of Cane River

http://ulpress.org
University of Louisiana at Lafayette Press
P.O. Box 43558
Lafayette, LA 70504-3558

Printed in Canada on acid-free paper

Library of Congress Cataloging-in-Publication Data

Names: Moran, Joseph Anthony, author, photographer.
Title: That was then : memories of Cane River / Joseph Anthony Moran.
Description: Lafayette : University of Louisiana at Lafayette Press, 2017.
Identifiers: LCCN 2017025956 | ISBN 9781946160065
Subjects: LCSH: Cane River Region (La.)--History--Pictorial works. |
   Natchitoches (La.)--History--Pictorial works. | Creoles--Louisiana--Cane
   River Region (La.)--Pictorial works. | Community life--Louisiana--Cane
   River Region (La.)--Pictorial works.
Classification: LCC F379.N2 M67 2017 | DDC 976.3/65--dc23
LC record available at https://lccn.loc.gov/2017025956

THAT WAS THEN
Memories of Cane River

———— ⋊⋉ ————

JOSEPH ANTHONY MORAN

UNIVERSITY OF LOUISIANA AT LAFAYETTE PRESS
2017

Preface

I made my first photographs on Cane River over forty years ago. They were pictures of strangers, made with a Polaroid instant camera. Snapshots of country people — humble folk going about their modest lives — that I encountered sitting on porches, tending their gardens, or working in their yards. Driving along back roads on visits from my home in Houston I was exploring the countryside, searching for inspiration for my paintings and drawings. The people, landscape, flora, fauna, rural buildings, and objects I photographed would be juxtaposed later in compositions I would create in my studio.

At the time the photos were merely taken as a utilitarian exercise. Eventually, I retired the Polaroid camera and acquired a 35 mm and a medium format camera, whose negatives allowed me to make larger and crisper images to work from. I began to develop and print my own photographs in makeshift darkrooms. Concurrently, I became increasingly familiar with Cane River people and their lifestyle and traditions. I was especially drawn to the older people whose quiet dignity, both in spirit and facial features, rendered a character I found appealing. The photos over time evolved into more than reference tools for my art. Many of them stood alone as works in their own right.

Having been enamored of the place since a child, I increasingly came to recognize how unique Cane River was and how much its spirit intrigued and haunted me. I decided to move there to become more deeply entrenched in the environment and the culture. I wanted to document in some small way my view of a community that was so integral to my make up. In excess of twenty years I sought to express my reverence for the place — the home of my ancestors — by photographing average inhabitants, folk practitioners and practices, community life and family.

Here I have gleaned from hundreds of images a few that I hope somehow convey a semblance of the community's essence during the years that I spent there. I have selected photos of people I especially connected with, those who trusted me to impose on their lives, some of whom became my friends, many who are no longer living, and of course my family.

Joseph Moran, October, 2016

About Cane River

Reputedly the oldest American settlement founded by and for people of color, Isle Brevelle — more commonly known as Cane River — originated in the late-eighteenth century as a result of the union of an enslaved African woman, Marie Thérèse Coin-Coin, and a French merchant, Claude-Thomas-Pierre Metoyer. This couple and their Franco-African offspring — through hard work, perseverance, and foresight — established a settlement that was unique in the confines of early America.

Marie Thérèse bought her and her children's freedom while she acquired large tracts of undeveloped land that she transformed into an enormously productive plantation known as Yucca (now Melrose). The family accrued abundant material wealth and was accorded a high social status rarely attained by people of color in those times.

The eldest of the children, Nicolas Augustin, envisioned the community as an exclusive haven where his family and other free Creoles of color could nurture their unique culture, free from the racial pressures and influences of the dominant white society. Nicolas established St. Augustine Church in 1803 as the center of religious and social activity. It remains today the nucleus around which the culture thrives.

Cane River people have developed folk customs that distinguish them from other communities in Louisiana and the nation. Close ties to the land and the river prevail. Crop farming, cattle raising, vegetable gardening, hunting, and fishing are practiced to some degree by many. Once prevalent customs such as sassafras gathering for gumbo filé, red pepper grinding for home bottling, and communal hog butchering continue to decline, however.

Cane River remains home to most who have ancestral or familial ties to it, whether they reside there or in other places. Many who have left return periodically to reconnect with its special spirit.

Cane River
The People, The Place

——)(——

Photographs

1

Neal Monette, Farmer, Raconteur

2

Creole Belle, Daphne Delphin at Badin Roque House

3

Young Angler, Matthew Moran

4

Cane River Swimming Hole

5

Boy and Man at Fishing Pier

6

Horace Christophe, Master Angler, Hunter, and Trapper

7

Young Squirrell Hunters with Bounty

8

Norah Sers Jr. with Rabbit Kill

9

Andy Bynog, Herbal Healer

10

King Cotton

11

Boy in Cotton Patch

12

Camellia Monette, Filé and Pepper Maker

13

Cayenne Peppers Being Strung for Drying

14

Jerry Jones Gathering Sassafras Leaves for Gumbo Filé

15

Mrs. Clara Jones Sorting Sassafras Leaves for Filé Grinding

16

Women Cooking for a Communal Meal

17

Bride and Grandfather Wedding Dance

18

Wedding Reception at St. Augustine Church Hall

19

Ring Bearer Making a Toast

20

Young People Socializing at Wedding Reception

21

Dancers at Wedding Reception

22

Dancing Couple at Wedding Reception

23

Pig Butchering – Going to the Kill

24

Pig Butchering – Stabbing the Heart of a Shoat

25

Pig Butchering – Men Scraping Skin of a Slaughtered Shoat

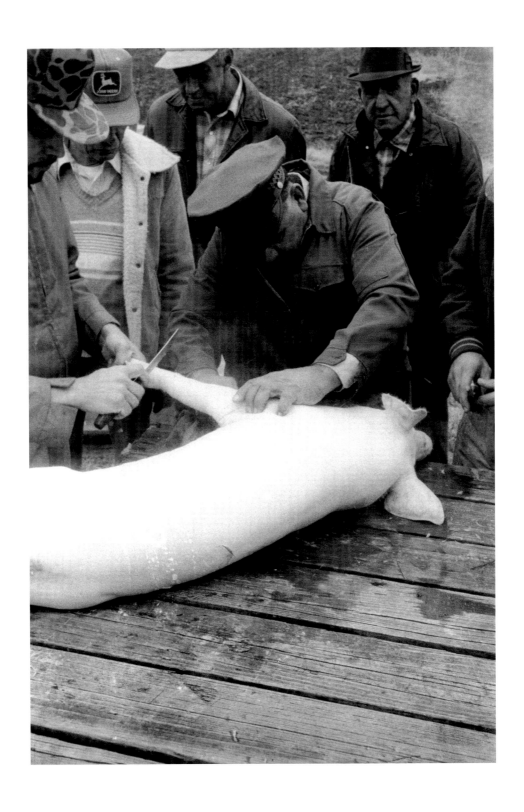

26

Pig Butchering – Bleeding a Shoat for Blood Sausage

27

Pig Butchering – Hanging Shoat

28

Severed Head of Pig

29

Sides of Pork Hang Inside the Kitchen of Neal and Roberta Monette After Butchering

30

Kirk Hall, The Friendly Escape at Dusk

31

Signs at Wood Hall, The Friendly Place

32

Wood Antee, Proprietor of "Wood's," The Friendly Place

33

Alphonse and Raymond Metoyer, Proprietors of Buh Buh's Cocktail Lounge

34

Alphonse "Buh Buh" Metoyer Outside His Night Club "Buh Buh's"

35

Jack o' Cott, Cowboy, Magnolia Plantation

36

Isaac Dupree, Cowboy

37

Isaac Dupre, Cowboy

38

Young Boy Playing Cowboy

39

Home Devotional Shrine of Mrs. Veronica Colson

40

Altar Boy, Thomas Roque Jr.

41

First Communicants

42

Procession Before Mass at St. Augustine Church with Portrait of Its Founder in Background

43

First Communion Ritual

44

May Queen Near Tomb of Grand Peré Augustin Metoyer

45

Funeral Procession to St. Augustine Church Graveyard

46

Congregants at a Cane River Baptism

47

Cane River Baptism

48

Woman After Being Baptized in Cane River

49

Statue of The Blessed Virgin Mary in a Resident's Yard

50

Woman Cleaning Graveyard in Preparation for All Saint's Day

51

Graveyard Candlelight Vigil, All Saint's Day

52

Candlelight Vigil at a Family Member's Grave, All Saint's Day

53

Candlelight Vigil, All Saint's Day

54

Spider Lilies at Badin Roque House

55

Madame Tina St. Ville, Retired Schoolteacher

56

Earvin LaCour, Master Faux Finishes Painter and Artist

57

Frances "Foosie" Balthazar at Garden Fence

58

Armela Rachal Before Her Vanity

59

Mama Lair LaCour, Doll and Quilt Maker

60

Domestic Fowl Behind a Farmhouse

61

Clementine "Tee Bay" Hunter, Renowned Artist

62

Artist Clementine Hunter Outside Her Home and Studio

63

Michael "Mickey" Moran, Oral Historian and Conversationalist, at the Badin Roque House

64

Mrs. Frances Meziere at the Fall Church Fair

65

Tony Moran, Cowboy, Chauffeur and Tenant Farmer, Magnolia Plantation

66

Mallory Jones with Spider Lilies

67

Reveler at Fall Church Fair

68

Revelers at Fall Church Fair

69

Azenor Sers, Herbalist, in His Yard

70

Farmhouse Bedroom

71

Interior of a Farmhouse with Occupant

72

Boy at Fence

Acknowledgments

I would like to thank the following people and institutions for their valued support of my photographic efforts regarding the Cane River community:

My beloved wife Judith and my children Jenny, Annie, and Max
Dr. Hiram "Pete" Gregory, anthropologist, Northwestern State University
Allison Peña, anthropologist, Jean Lafitte National Historic Park, National Park Service
Maida Owens, director, Louisiana Folklife Program, Louisiana Division of the Arts
Rick Olivier, photographer, mentor, and friend
The St. Augustine Historical Society
The Louisiana Endowment for the Humanities
Contemporary Arts Center, New Orleans
University of Louisiana at Lafayette Press
Every person whose image appears in this collection of photographs